SELECTED P

ROBERT B

Robert Burns (1759–96) entered the world on 25 January as the first of William Burnes and Agnes Brown's seven children (four boys and three girls). Burnes was not a successful farmer and had to struggle with harsh land and demanding factors first at Mount Oliphant and then at Lochlie farm at Tarbolton. Nevertheless, he aimed to give Robert and his brother Gilbert a decent education, sending them to village schools and making arrangements for Robert to spend some of the summer months studying French and Mathematics with his former teacher as tutor. By the age of 15 Burns was widely read in English literature and considered something of a 'prodigy' in French, but it seems likely that hard labour on the farm weakened his heart and eventually contributed to an early death.

Forming a Bachelors' club and debating society at Tarbolton, young Robert became a Freemason, worked as a flax dresser in Irvine and enjoyed an active social and sexual life. He began to write poems, inspired to use Scots by the work of Robert Fergusson. His father's illness, his debts, and a court case over his rent arrears brought the poet back to Lochlie and when William Burnes died in 1784, Robert and Gilbert took up a farm at nearby Mossgiel and found themselves supporting the family. By this time Burns was involved with Betty Paton, by whom he had a daughter, and Jean Armour was also pregnant. (She was to bear him two pairs of twins before he eventually married her in 1788.) During these years (1784–6) Burns wrote some his most famous poems, including many epistles to various friends, his attacks on religious hypocrisy 'Holy Willie's Prayer', his celebration of Rabelaisian energy in 'The Holy Fair' and 'The Jolly Beggars' and his subtle but scathing satire on social injustice 'The Twa Dogs'. Creative or not, these were difficult and exhausting years and faced with local scandal, nervous strain, unrewarding hard labour and rising debt, Burns considered emigrating to Jamaica. The success of his first collection, *Poems, Chiefly in the Scottish Dialect* (1786) did much to change his mind. This first 'Kilmarnock Edition' sold out and a revised 'Edinburgh Edition' followed in 1787 to even greater acclaim, with an American edition published the following year.

Burns spent the winters of 1786–7 and 1787–8 in Edinburgh, lionised by society and the literary establishment, if largely misunderstood and sentimentalised by them as a 'heaven-taught ploughman'. Despite his literary success, however, Burns found it difficult to get any money from his Edinburgh publisher, William Creech, and was still in need of a patron or a job. Having spent the summer months of these years touring the Borders and the Highlands, he took an interest in old Scots songs and this led to his writing, collecting and rewriting songs for Johnson's *Scots Musical Museum* (1787–1803) and *Thomson's Select Scottish Airs* (1793–1818), a major task to which he devoted himself for the rest of his life. The poet took up farming again at Ellisland in the summer of 1788, and set about training to be an Excise Officer. The farm at Ellisland was not a success, and in 1791 Burns moved to Dumfries where he took up the post of Excise Officer. These last years were times of considerable political and social unrest throughout Britain and in 1795 severe shortages and food riots broke out in Dumfries. Burns's health was as uncertain as his finances. The poet's weak heart was exacerbated by the medicines of the day and, fevered and fearing for the future of his family, he died at home on 21 July 1796 at the age of 37.

SELECTED POEMS

Robert Burns

I

CANONGATE POCKET CLASSICS

First published as a Pocket Classic in 2001 by
Canongate Books Ltd, 14 High Street, Edinburgh
EHI ITE.

Selection and biographical note copyright © Roderick Watson, 2001. The glosses for the poems
are included by kind permission of Andrew Noble
and Patrick Scott Hogg, editors of *The Canongate
Burns*.

10 9 8 7 6 5 4 3 2 1

The publishers gratefully acknowledge general
subsidy from the Scottish Arts Council towards
the Canongate Classics and Pocket Classics series.

Typeset in 10pt Plantin by Hewer Text Ltd,
Edinburgh.

Printed and bound by Omnia Books, Glasgow.

CANONGATE CLASSICS
Series Editor: Roderick Watson
Editorial Board: John Pick, Cairns Craig,
Dorothy McMillan

ISBN I 84195 155 2

www.canongate.net

Contents

The Twa Dogs: A Tale

'Twas in that place o' *Scotland*'s isle
That bears the name of auld King COIL,   old, Kyle
Upon a bonie day in June,   bonny
When wearing thro' the afternoon,
Twa Dogs, that were na thrang at hame,   two, not busy, home
Forgather'd ance upon a time.   met by chance, once

The first I'll name, they ca'd him *Caesar*,   called
Was keepet for his Honor's pleasure: kept
His hair, his size, his mouth, his lugs,   ears
Shew'd he was nane o' Scotland's dogs;   none
But whalpet some place far abroad,   pupped
Whare sailors gang to fish for Cod.   where, go

His locked, letter'd, braw brass-collar
Shew'd him the *gentleman* an' *scholar*;
But tho' he was o' high degree,
The fient a pride, na pride had he;   fiend, no
But wad hae spent an hour caressan,   would have

I

Ev'n wi' a Tinkler-gipsey's *messan*;   mongrel

At *Kirk* or *Market*, *Mill* or *Smiddie*,   smithy

Nae tawtied *tyke*, tho' e'er sae duddie,   matted cur,
                                                    so ragged

But he wad stan't, as glad to see him,   would have
                                                stood

An' stroan't on stanes an' hillocks wi' him.   pissed,
                                                       stones

The tither was a *ploughman's collie*,

A rhyming, ranting, raving billie,   fellow/
                                            character

Wha for his friend an' comrade had him,   who

And in his freaks had *Luath* ca'd him,

After some dog in *Highland Sang*,

Was made lang syne, Lord knows how lang.   long ago

He was a gash an' faithfu' *tyke*,   wise, dog

As ever lap a sheugh or dyke!   leapt, ditch,
                                       stone wall

His honest, sonsie, baws'nt face   friendly,
                                          white marks

Ay gat him friends in ilka place;   always got,
                                           every

His *breast* was white, his touzie *back*   shaggy

Weel clad wi' coat o' glossy black;   well
                                             covered

His gawsie tail, wi' upward curl,   fine/full

Hung owre his hurdies wi' a swirl.   over,
                                            buttocks

Nae doubt but they were fain o' ither,   no, fond of
                                                each other

And unco pack an' thick thegither;   kept secrets/
                                            confidential

Wi' social *nose* whyles snuff'd an' snowcket;   whiles,
                                                        sniffed

Whyles mice an' moudiewurks they howcket;　*whiles, moles, dug for*

Whyles scour'd awa' in lang excursion,　*whiles, long*

An' worry'd ither in *diversion*;

Till tir'd at last wi' monie a farce,　*many*

They sat them down upon their arse,

An' there began a lang digression　*long*

About the *lords o' the creation.*

CAESAR

I've aften wonder'd, honest *Luath*,　*often*

What sort o' life poor dogs like you have;

An' when the *gentry's* life I saw,

What way poor bodies liv'd ava.　*at all*

Our *Laird* gets in his racked rents,　*extortionate payments in kind, dues*

His coals, his kane, an' a' his stents:

He rises when he likes himsel;

His flunkies answer at the bell;　*servants*

He ca's his coach; he ca's his horse;　*calls*

He draws a bonie, silken purse,　*carries*

As lang's my *tail*, whare thro' the steeks,　*long as, where, stiches*

The yellow, letter'd *Geordie* keeks.　*guinea (King's head) peeps*

Frae morn to een it's nought but toiling, — from, evening, nothing

At baking, roasting, frying, boiling;

An' tho' the gentry first are steghan, — cramming

Yet ev'n the *ha' folk* fill their peghan — hall (servants), stomach

Wi' sauce, ragouts, an sic like trashtrie, — such like rubbish

That's little short o' downright wastrie: — wastage

Our *Whipper-in*, wee, blastit wonner, — small, blasted wonder

Poor, worthless elf, it eats a dinner,

Better than onie *Tenant-man* — any

His Honor has in a' the lan': — all the land

An' what poor *Cot-folk* pit their painch in, — put, paunch

I own it's past my comprehension.

LUATH

Trowth, *Caesar*, whyles they're fash'd eneugh: — sometimes, bothered

A *Cotter* howckan in a sheugh, — farm labourer, digging, ditch

Wi' dirty stanes biggan a dyke, — stones, building, stone wall

Bairan a quarry, an' sic like, — clearing, such

Himsel, a wife, he thus sustains,

A smytrie o' wee duddie weans, — number, small ragged children

An' nought but his han'-daurk, to keep — hands' work

Them right an' tight in *thack an' raep*. — snug, thatch, rope

An' when they meet wi' sair disasters, — sore

Like loss o' health or want o' masters,

Ye maist wad think, a wee touch langer, most would, longer

An' they maun starve o' cauld and hunger: should, cold

But how it comes, I never kend yet, knew

They're maistly wonderfu' contented; mostly

An' buirdly chiels, an' clever hizzies, stout lads, girls

Are bred in sic a way as this is. such

CAESAR

But then to see how ye're neglecket, neglected

How huff'd, an' cuff'd, an' disrespecket! scolded, slapped, disrespected

Lord man, our gentry care as little

For *delvers*, *ditchers*, an' sic cattle; labourers, diggers, such

They gang as saucy by poor folk, go, smugly would,

As I wad by a stinkan brock. badger

I've notic'd, on our Laird's *court-day*,

(An' monie a time my heart's been wae), many, sad short of money

Poor tenant bodies, scant o' cash,

How they maun thole a *Factor's* snash: would suffer, abuse

He'll stamp an' threaten, curse an' swear

He'll *apprehend* them, *poind* their gear; seize & sell their goods

While they maun staun', wi' aspect humble, must stand

An' hear it a', an' fear an' tremble! all

I see how folk live that hae riches;   have
But surely poor-folk maun be wretches!   must

LUATH

They're nae sae wretched's ane wad think: not so, as
                                                         one would
Tho' constantly on poortith's brink,   poverty's
They're sae accustom'd wi' the sight,   so
The view o't gies them little fright.   gives

Then chance an' fortune are sae guided,   so
They're ay in less or mair provided;   always,
                                                         more
An' tho' fatigu'd wi' close employment,
A blink o' rest's a sweet enjoyment.

The dearest comfort o' their lives,
Their grushie weans an' faithfu' wives;   thriving
                                                         children
The *prattling things* are just their pride,
That sweetens a' their fire-side.

An' whyles twalpennie worth o' *nappy*   sometimes,
                                                         ale
Can mak the bodies unco happy: folk, very
They lay aside their private cares,
To mind the Kirk an' State affairs;
They'll talk o' *patronage* an' *priests*,
Wi' kindling fury i' their breasts,

Or tell what new taxation's comin,

An' ferlie at the folk in Lon'on.   *wonder*

As bleak-fac'd Hallowmass returns,   *festival of All-Saints*

They get the jovial, rantan *Kirns*,   *harvest homes*

When *rural life*, of ev'ry station,

Unite in common recreation;

Love blinks, Wit slaps, an' social Mirth

Forgets there's *Care* upo' the earth.

That *merry day* the year begins,

They bar the door on frosty win's;   *winds*

The nappy reeks wi' mantling ream,   *ale, foaming froth*

An' sheds a heart-inspiring steam;

The luntan pipe, an' sneeshin mill,   *smoking, snuff box*

Are handed round wi' right guid will;   *good*

The cantie, auld folks, crackan crouse,   *jolly old, chatting, cheerful ones,*

The young anes rantan thro' the house —   *running*

My heart has been sae fain to see them,   *so content*

That I for joy hae *barket* wi' them.   *have barked*

Still it's owre true that ye hae said   *over, have*

Sic game is now owre aften play'd;   *such a, over often*

There's monie a creditable *stock*   *many*

O' decent, honest, fawsont folk,   *respectable*

Are riven out baith root an' branch,   thrown out by
                                              force, both
Some rascal's pridefu' greed to quench,
Wha thinks to knit himsel the faster   who
In favor wi' some *gentle Master*,
Wha, aiblins thrang a *parliamentin'*,   who, maybe
                                              crowd
For *Britain's guid* his saul indentin' –   good, soul
                                              engaged

CAESAR

Haith, lad, ye little ken about it: an exclamation,
                                              know
For Britain's guid! guid faith! I doubt it. good
Say rather, gaun as PREMIERS lead him: go
An' saying *aye* or *no's* they bid him:
At Operas an' Plays parading,
Mortgaging, gambling, masquerading:
Or maybe, in a frolic daft,
To HAGUE or CALAIS takes a waft,
To mak *a tour* an' tak a whirl,
To learn *bon ton*, an' see the worl'.   Fr. good
                                              breeding

There, at VIENNA or VERSAILLES,
He rives his father's auld entails;   splits, old
Or by MADRID he taks the rout,   road
To thrum guittarres an' fecht wi' *nowt*;   strum guitars,
                                              fight with bulls
Or down *Italian Vista* startles,   courses

Whore-hunting amang groves o' myrtles: among
Then bowses drumlie *German-water*,   drinks
                                         muddy
To mak himsel look fair an' fatter,
An' clear the consequential sorrows,
Love-gifts of Carnival Signioras.
For Britain's guid! for her destruction!
Wi' dissipation, feud an' faction!

LUATH

Hech man! dear sirs! is that the gate   way
They waste sae monie a braw estate!   so many
Are we sae foughten an' harass'd   so troubled
For gear ta gang that gate at last!   wealth to go

O would they stay aback frae courts,   away from
An' please themsels wi' countra sports,   country
It wad for ev'ry ane be better,   would,
                                       every one
The *Laird*, the *Tenant*, an' the *Cotter*!
For thae frank, rantan, ramblan billies,   they,
                                            fellows
Fient haet o' them's ill-hearted fellows;   few of them
                                             are
Except for breakin o' their timmer,   timber
Or speakin lightly o' their *limmer*,   mistress
Or shootin of a hare or moor-cock,
The ne'er-a-bit they're ill to poor folk.

But will ye tell me, master Caesar,
Sure *great folk's* life's a life o' pleasure?
Nae cauld nor hunger e'er can steer them,   no cold,
                                                    touch
The vera thought o't need na fear them.   very, not

CAESAR

Lord, man, were ye but whyles whare I am,   whiles
                                                    where
The *Gentles*, ye wad ne'er envy them!   would

It's true, they need na starve or sweat,   not
Thro' Winter's cauld, or Simmer's heat;   cold,
                                                    summer's
They've nae sair-work to craze their banes,   no sore
                                                    work, bones
An' fill *auld-age* wi' grips an' granes: old-age, gripes &
                                                    groans
But *human bodies* are sic fools,   such
For a' their Colledges an' Schools,
That when nae *real* ills perplex them,   no
They *mak* enow themsels to vex them;
An' ay the less they hae to sturt them,   always,
                                                    have, fret
In like proportion, less will hurt them.

A countra fellow at the pleugh,   country,
                                                    plough
His *acre's* till'd, he's right eneugh;   well
                                                    enough
A countra girl at her wheel,   country
Her *dizzen's* done, she's unco weel;   dozen's,
                                                    very well
But Gentlemen, an' Ladies warst,

Wi' ev'n down *want o' wark* they're curst: work
They loiter, lounging, lank an' lazy;
Tho' deil-haet ails them, yet uneasy: nothing
Their days insipid, dull an' tasteless;
Their nights unquiet, lang an' restless.   long

An' ev'n their sports, their balls an' races,
Their galloping thro' public places,
There's sic parade, sic pomp an' art,   such
The joy can scarcely reach the heart.

The *Men* cast out in *party-matches*,   compete
Then sowther a' in deep debauches;   patch up
Ae night they're mad wi' drink an' whoring,   one
Niest day their life is past enduring.   next

The *Ladies* arm-in-arm in clusters,
As great an' gracious a' as sisters;   all
But hear their *absent thoughts* o' ither,
They're a' run deils an' jads thegither.   downright, together
Whyles, owre the wee bit cup an' platie,   whiles, over, plate
They sip the *scandal-potion* pretty;
Or lee-lang nights, wi' crabbet leuks   live-long, bad tempered looks
Pore owre the devil's *pictur'd beuks*;   over, books
Stake on a chance a farmer's stackyard,
An' cheat like onie *unhang'd blackguard*.   any, villain

There's some exceptions, man an' woman;
But this is Gentry's life in common.

By this, the sun was out o' sight,
An' darker gloamin brought the night;   fading
                                          twilight
The *bum-clock* humm'd wi' lazy drone;   beetle
The kye stood rowtin i' the loan;   cattle,
                                          lowing,
                                          field

When up they gat, an' shook their lugs,   got, ears
Rejoic'd they were na *men*, but *dogs*; not
An' each took aff his several way,   went his
                                          different
Resolv'd to meet some ither day.   other

To a Louse
On Seeing One on a Lady's Bonnet at Church

Ha! whare ye gaun, ye crowlan ferlie! *(where, going, crawling wonder)*
Your impudence protects you sairly: *(very well)*
I canna say but ye strunt rarely *(cannot, strut confidently)*
     Owre *gauze* and *lace*, *(over)*
Tho' faith, I fear ye dine but sparely *(eat little)*
     On sic a place. *(such)*

Ye ugly, creepan, blastet wonner, *(blasted wonder)*
Detested, shunn'd by saunt an' sinner, *(saint)*
How daur ye set your fit upon her — *(dare, foot)*
     Sae fine a *Lady*! *(so)*
Gae somewhere else and seek your dinner *(go)*
     On some poor body.

Swith, in some beggar's haffet squattle: *(away!, temples, squat)*
There ye may creep, and sprawl, and sprattle, *(scramble)*
Wi' ither kindred, jumping cattle, *(other)*
     In shoals and nations;
Whare *horn* nor *bane* ne'er daur unsettle *(where, bone, dare)*
     Your thick plantations.

13

Now haud you there, ye're out o' sight,   hold

Below the fatt'rels, snug an' tight,   ribbon-ends

Na, faith ye yet! ye'll no be right,   no, confound you

       Till ye've got on it,

The vera tapmost, tow'ring height   very topmost

       O' *Miss's bonnet*.   hat

My sooth! right bauld ye set your nose out,   bold

As plump an' grey as onie grozet: any gooseberry

O for some rank, mercurial rozet,   mercury pasted rosin

       Or fell, red smeddum,   deadly powder

I'd gie ye sic a hearty dose o't,   give

       Wad dress your droddum!   would, backside

I wad na been surpris'd to spy   would not

You on an auld wife's *flainen toy*;   old flannel cap

Or aiblins some bit duddie boy,   perhaps, small ragged

       On's *wylecoat*;   flannel vest

But Miss's fine *Lunardi*, fye!   balloon-shaped hat

       How daur ye do't?   dare

O *Jenny*, dinna toss your head,   do not

An' set your beauties a' abroad!   abroad/on view

Ye little ken what cursèd speed   know

       The blastie's makin!   damned thing's

Thae *winks* an' *finger-ends*, I dread,
      Are notice takin!

*they – who
see and
print*

O wad some Pow'r the giftie gie us
To *see oursels as ithers see us*!
It wad frae monie a blunder free us,
      An' foolish notion:
What airs in dress an' gait wad lea'e us,
      An' ev'n Devotion!

*would, gift
give*

*others
would from
many*

*appearance,
would leave*

To a Mouse
On Turning her up in her Nest with the Plough, November 1785

Wee, sleekit, cowrin, tim'rous *beastie*,
small, sleek

O, what a panic's in thy breastie!
breast

Thou need na start awa sae hasty
away, so hasty,

      Wi' bickering brattle!
scurry

I wad be laith to rin an' chase thee,
would, loth, run

      Wi' murdering *pattle*!
a wooden plough-scraper

I'm truly sorry Man's dominion

Has broken Nature's social union,

An' justifies that ill opinion

      Which makes thee startle

At me, thy poor, earth-born companion

      An' *fellow mortal*!

I doubt na, whyles, but thou may thieve;
not, sometimes

What then? poor beastie, thou maun live!
must

A *daimen icker* in a *thrave*
one ear of corn in 24 sheaves

      'S a sma' request;

I'll get a blessin wi' the lave,
remainder

      An' never miss't!

17

Thy wee-bit *housie*, too, in ruin!   small, house/nest

Its silly wa's the win's are strewin!   walls, winds

An' naething, now, to big a new ane,   nothing, build, new one

        O' foggage green!   thick winter grass

An' bleak *December's win's* ensuin,   winds

        Baith snell an' keen!   both bitter, biting cold

Thou saw the fields laid bare an' waste,

An' weary *Winter* comin fast,

An' cozie here, beneath the blast,   cosy

        Thou thought to dwell,

Till crash! the cruel *coulter* past   plough blade

        Out thro' thy cell.

That wee bit heap o' leaves an' stibble,   small, stubble

Has cost thee monie a weary nibble!   many

Now thou's turned out, for a' thy trouble,

        But house or hald,   without, holding

To thole the Winter's *sleety dribble*,   endure, drizzle

        An' *cranreuch* cauld!   hoar-frost cold

But Mousie, thou art no thy lane,   not alone

In proving *foresight* may be vain:

The best-laid schemes o' *Mice* an' *Men*

        Gang aft agley,   go often wrong

An' lea'e us nought but grief an' pain,   leave

        For promis'd joy!

Still thou art blest, compared wi' me!
The *present* only toucheth thee:
But Och! I backward cast my e'e,
    On prospects drear!
An' *forward*, tho' I canna *see*,
    I *guess* an' *fear*!

cannot

Address to the Deil

O Prince! O Chief of many thronèd pow'rs!
That led th' embattl'd seraphim to war.
                                        Milton

O Thou! whatever title suit thee —
Auld Hornie, Satan, Nick, or Clootie —   old, cloven-
                                                hoofed
Wha in yon cavern grim an' sootie,   who, filled
                                                with soot
    Clos'd under hatches,
Spairges about the brunstane cootie,   splashes,
                                                brimstone dish
    To scaud poor wretches!   scald

Hear me, *auld Hangie*, for a wee,   old hangman,
                                                while
An' let poor *damnèd bodies* be;
I'm sure sma' pleasure it can gie,   give
    Ev'n to a *deil*,   devil
To skelp an' scaud poor dogs like me   hit/slap,
                                                scald
    An' hear us squeel!

Great is thy pow'r an' great thy fame;
Far kend, an' noted is thy name;
An' tho' yon *lowan heugh's* thy hame,
       Thou travels far;
An' faith! thou's neither lag, nor lame,
       Nor blate nor scaur.

Whyles, ranging like a roarin lion,
For prey, a' holes an' corners tryin;
Whyles, on the strong-wing'd Tempest flyin,
       Tirlan the *Kirks*;
Whyles, in the human bosom pryin,
       Unseen thou lurks.

I've heard my rev'rend *Graunie* say,
In lanely glens ye like to stray;
Or, where auld ruin'd castles grey
       Nod to the moon,
Ye fright the nightly wand'rer's way
       Wi' eldritch croon.

When twilight did my *Graunie* summon,
To say her pray'rs, douce, honest woman!
Aft yont the dyke she's heard you bumman,
       Wi' eerie drone;

*Glosses (right margin):*

- known
- moaning, hollow, home
- backward
- bashful, afraid
- sometimes
- stripping – attacking
- grannie
- lonely
- old
- unearthly eerie moan
- grannie
- sober/ prudent
- away beyond

Or, rustlin, thro' the boortries coman,   alder trees
        Wi' heavy groan.   coming

Ae dreary, windy, winter night,   one
The stars shot down wi' sklentan light,   slanting
Wi' you mysel, I gat a fright: got
        Ayont the lough,   beyond, loch
Ye, like a *rash-buss*, stood in sight,   bunch of rushes
         Wi' waving sugh: moan

The cudgel in my nieve did shake,   fist
Each bristl'd hair stood like a stake;
When wi' an eldritch, stoor *quaick*, *quaick*,   unearthly harsh, duck quack
        Amang the springs,   among
Awa ye squatter'd like a *drake*,   away, a noisy take-off
        On whistling wings.

Let *Warlocks* grim, an' wither'd *Hags*,
Tell how wi' you, on ragweed nags,   ragwort
They skim the muirs an' dizzy crags,   moors, high peaks
        Wi' wicked speed;
And in kirk-yards renew their leagues,
        Owre howket dead.   over those raised from the grave

Thence, countra wives, wi' toil an' pain,   country

May plunge an' plunge the *kirn* in vain;   churn

For Och! the yellow treasure's taen   taken

    By witching skill;

An' dawtit, twal-pint *Hawkie's* gaen   petted, 12-pint cow has gone

    As yell's the Bill.   dry, bull

Thence, mystic knots mak great abuse

On *Young-Guidmen*, fond, keen an' croose;   husbands, over confident

When the best *warklum* i' the house,   work-tool, penis

    By cantraip wit,   magic/evil

Is instant made no worth a louse,

    Just at the bit.   stopped before ejaculation

When thowes dissolve the snawy hoord,   thaws, snowy hoard

An' float the jinglin icy boord,   water's surface

Then, *Water-kelpies* haunt the foord,   imaginary water-spirits, ford

    By your direction,

An' nighted Trav'llers are allur'd

    To their destruction.

An' aft your moss-traversing *Spunkies*   often, bog-, demons

Decoy the wight that late an' drunk is: fellow

The bleezan, curst, mischievous monkies
      Delude his eyes,
Till in some miry slough he sunk *is, dirty hole*
      Ne'er mair to rise. *more*

When MASONS' mystic *word* an' *grip*
In storms an' tempests raise you up,
Some cock or cat your rage maun stop, *shall*
      Or, strange to tell!
The *youngest Brother* ye wad whip *would*
      Aff straught to *Hell*. *off straight*

Lang syne in *Eden's* bonie yard, *long ago, bony garden*
When youthfu' lovers first were pair'd,
An' all the Soul of Love they shar'd,
      The raptur'd hour,
Sweet on the fragrant flow'ry swaird, *grassy edge*
      In shady bow'r:

Then you, ye auld, snick-drawing dog! *old, noisy door opener*
Ye cam to Paradise incog, *came, disguised*
An' play'd on man a cursed brogue *trick*
      (Black be your fa'!), *fall*
An' gied the infant warld a shog, *gave, world, shake*
      'Maist ruin'd a'. *almost*

D'ye mind that day when in a bizz   flurry/ bustle
Wi' reeket duds, an' reestet gizz,   smoky clothes, scorched wig
Ye did present your smoutie phiz   obscene/ ugly face
          'Mang better folk;
An' sklented on the *man of Uzz*   squinted at Job
          Your spitefu' joke?

An' how ye gat him i' your thrall,   got, spell
An' brak him out o' house an' hal',   broke
While scabs an' blotches did him gall,
          Wi' bitter claw;
An' lows'd his ill-tongu'd wicked *Scawl* —   slackened, scolding wife
          Was warst ava?   worst of all

But a' your doings to rehearse,
Your wily snares an' fechtin fierce,   fighting
Sin' that day MICHAEL did you pierce
          Down to this time,
Wad ding a *Lallan* tongue, or *Erse*,   would, beat, Lowland Scots, Irish
          In Prose or Rhyme.

An' now, auld *Cloots*, I ken ye're thinkan,   old, know
A certain Bardie's rantin, drinkin,
Some luckless hour will send him linkan,   hurrying
          To your black pit;   Hell

But, faith! he'll turn a corner jinkin,   dodging
       An' cheat you yet.

But fare-you-weel, auld *Nickie-ben*!   old
O wad ye tak a thought an' men'!   would, mend
Ye aiblins might — I dinna ken —   perhaps, do not know
       Still hae a *stake*:   have
I'm wae to think upo' yon den,   sad
       Ev'n for your sake.

Address to a Haggis

Fair fa' your honest, sonsie face, *good luck / to, cheerful*
Great Chieftain o' the Puddin-race!
Aboon them a' ye tak your place, *above*
    Painch, tripe, or thairm: *paunch, guts*
Weel are ye wordy of a *grace* *well*
    As lang's my arm. *long as*

The groaning trencher there ye fill,
Your hurdies like a distant hill, *buttocks*
Your *pin* wad help to mend a mill *skewer / would*
    In time o' need,
While thro' your pores the dews distil
    Like amber bead.

His knife see Rustic-labour dight, *wipe*
An' cut ye up wi' ready slight, *skill*
Trenching your gushing entrails bright,
    Like onie ditch; *any*
And then, O what a glorious sight,
    Warm-reekin, rich! *-steaming*

Then, horn for horn, they stretch an' strive: eating with a horn-spoon

Deil tak the hindmost, on they drive, devil take the *leftovers*

Till a' their weel-swall'd kytes belyve well-swollen stomachs

    Are bent like drums; eventually

Then auld Guidman, maist like to rive, old goodman, most, burst

    Bethankit hums.

Is there that owre his French *ragout*, over

Or *olio* that wad staw a sow, would, fill up/bloat

Or *fricassee* wad mak her spew would make, throw up

    Wi' perfect sconner, disgust

Looks down wi' sneering, scornfu' view

    On sic a dinner? such

Poor devil! see him owre his trash, over

As feckless as a wither'd rash, feeble, rush

His spindle shank a guid whip-lash, thin leg, good

    His nieve a nit; fist, nut

Thro' bluidy flood or field to dash, bloody

    O how unfit!

But mark the Rustic, *haggis-fed*, country man

The trembling earth resounds his tread,

Clap in his walie nieve a blade,
    He'll make it whissle;
An' legs, an' arms, an' heads will sned
    Like taps o' thrissle.

Ye Pow'rs wha mak mankind your care,
And dish them out their bill o' fare,
Auld Scotland wants nae skinking ware,
    That jaups in luggies;
But, if ye wish her gratefu' prayer,
    Gie her a *Haggis*!

place, firm fist
whistle/cutting through air
cut off
tops of thistle
who make
old, no watery splashes in bowls
give

Holy Willie's Prayer

And send the Godly in a pet to pray.

Alexander Pope

O Thou that in the Heavens does dwell!
Wha, as it pleases best Thysel,   who, thyself
Sends ane to Heaven an' ten to Hell,   one
    A' for Thy glory!   all
And no for ony guid or ill   any good
    They've done before Thee. —

I bless and praise Thy matchless might,
When thousands Thou hast left in night,
That I am here before Thy sight,
    For gifts an' grace,
A burning and a shining light
    To a' this place. —

What was I, or my generation,
That I should get sic exaltation?   such

I, wha deserv'd most just damnation,　　　who
　　　　For broken laws
Sax thousand years ere my creation,　　　six
　　　　Thro' Adam's cause!

When from my mither's womb I fell,　　　mother's
Thou might hae plung'd me deep in hell,　　　have
To gnash my gooms, and weep, and wail,　　　gums
　　　　In burning lakes,
Whare damned devils roar and yell　　　where
　　　　Chain'd to their stakes. —

Yet I am here, a chosen sample,
To show Thy grace is great and ample:
I'm here a pillar o' Thy temple
　　　　Strong as a rock,
A guide, a ruler and example
　　　　To a' Thy flock. —

O Lord thou kens what zeal I bear,　　　knows
When drinkers drink, and swearers swear,
And singin' there, and dancin' here,
　　　　Wi' great an' sma';　　　small
For I am keepet by Thy fear,　　　kept
　　　　Free frae them a'. —　　　from, all

But yet — O Lord — confess I must —
At times I'm fash'd wi' fleshly lust;   troubled
And sometimes too, in warldly trust   worldly
     Vile Self gets in;
But Thou remembers we are dust,
     Defiled wi' sin. —

O Lord — yestreen — Thou kens —   last night, knows
        wi' Meg —
Thy pardon I sincerely beg!
O may't ne'er be a living plague,
     To my dishonour!
An' I'll ne'er lift a lawless leg
     Again upon her. —

Besides, I farther maun avow,   must
Wi' Leezie's lass, three times — I trow —
But, Lord, that Friday I was fou   full/drunk
     When I cam near her;   came
Or else, Thou kens, Thy servant true   knows
     Wad never steer her. —   would, meddle with

Maybe Thou lets this fleshly thorn
Buffet Thy servant e'en and morn,   evening
Lest he owre proud and high should turn,   over
     That he's sae gifted;   so

If sae, Thy han' maun e'en be borne
     Untill Thou lift it. —

so, hand
must

Lord, bless Thy chosen in this place,
For here Thou has a chosen race:
But God, confound their stubborn face,
     An' blast their name,
Wha bring Thy elders to disgrace
     An' open shame. —

who

Lord mind Gaun Hamilton's deserts!
He drinks, and swears, an' plays at cartes,
Yet has sae monie takin arts
     Wi' Great and Sma',
Frae God's ain priest the people's hearts
     He steals awa. —

Gavin

cards
so many
popular

small

from, own

away

And when we chasten'd him therefore,
Thou kens how he bred sic a splore,
And set the warld in a roar
     O' laughin at us:
Curse Thou his basket and his store,
     Kail an' potatoes. —

knows,
such, row

world

cabbage/
greens

Lord, hear my earnest cry and prayer
Against that Presbytry of Ayr!
Thy strong right hand, Lord, mak it bare
     Upon their heads!
Lord visit them, and dinna spare,   *do not*
     For their misdeeds!

O Lord my God, that glib-tongu'd Aiken!   *loose-*
My vera heart and flesh are quakin   *very*
To think how I sat, sweating, shaking,
     An' pish'd wi' dread,   *wet myself*
While Auld wi' hingin lip an' sneaking   *hanging, sneering*
     And hid his head!

Lord, in Thy day o' vengeance try him!
Lord visit him wha did employ him!   *who*
And pass not in Thy mercy by them,
     Nor hear their prayer;
But for Thy people's sake destroy them,
     An' dinna spare!   *do not*

But Lord, remember me and mine
Wi' mercies temporal and divine!
That I for grace an' gear may shine,
     Excell'd by nane!   *none*
And a' the glory shall be Thine!
     AMEN! AMEN!

Tam o' Shanter: A Tale

Of Brownyis and of Bogillis full is this Buke.
                                    Gawin Douglas

When chapman billies leave the street,   *pedlar*
                                            friends
And drouthy neebors, neebors meet,   *thirsty*
                                            neighbours
As market-days are wearing late,
An' folk begin to tak the gate;   *road/go home*
While we sit bousing at the nappy,   *drinking, ale*
And getting fou and unco happy,   *full/drunk, mighty*
We think na on the lang Scots miles,   *not, long*
The mosses, waters, slaps, and styles,   *bogs, pools, stiles*
That lie between us and our hame,   *home*
Whare sits our sulky sullen dame,   *where*
Gathering her brows like gathering storm,
Nursing her wrath to keep it warm.

    This truth fand honest *Tam o' Shanter*, *found*
As he frae Ayr ae night did canter,   *from, one*
(Auld Ayr, wham ne'er a town surpasses   *who/that*
For honest men and bonie lasses).

39

O *Tam!* had'st thou but been sae wise,   *so*

As taen thy ain wife *Kate's* advice!   *taken, own*

She tauld thee weel thou was a skellum,   *told, well, rogue*

A blethering, blustering, drunken blellum;   *chattering, babbling, idle talker*

That frae November till October,   *from*

Ae market-day thou was nae sober;   *one, not*

That ilka melder, wi' the miller,   *every meal, grinding*

Thou sat as lang as thou had siller;   *long, money*

That ev'ry naig was ca'd a shoe on,   *horse, shod*

The smith and thee gat roaring fou on;   *got, full/drunk*

That at the Lord's house, even on Sunday,

Thou drank wi' Kirkton Jean till Monday.

She prophesied that late or soon,

Thou would be found deep drown'd in Doon;

Or catch'd wi' warlocks in the mirk,   *wizards, dark*

By *Alloway's* auld, haunted kirk.   *old*

Ah, gentle dames! it gars me greet,   *makes, weep*

To think how mony counsels sweet,   *many*

How mony lengthen'd, sage advices,   *many*

The husband frae the wife despises!   *from*

But to our tale: — Ae market-night,   *one*

Tam had got planted unco right;   *mighty*

Fast by an ingle, bleezing finely,   fire, blazing

Wi' reaming swats, that drank divinely   foaming ale

And at his elbow, Souter *Johnny*,   cobbler

His ancient, trusty, drouthy crony;   drinking pal

Tam lo'ed him like a very brither —   loved, brother

They had been fou for weeks thegither!   full/drunk, together

The night drave on wi' sangs and clatter   drove, songs, chat

And ay the ale was growing better:

The landlady and *Tam* grew gracious,

Wi' favours, secret, sweet and precious:

The Souter tauld his queerest stories;   cobbler told

The landlord's laugh was ready chorus:

The storm without might rair and rustle,   roar

Tam did na mind the storm a whistle.   not

Care, mad to see a man sae happy,   so

E'en drown'd himsel amang the nappy: among, ale

As bees flee hame wi' lades o' treasure,   fly home, loads

The minutes wing'd their way wi' pleasure:

Kings may be blest, but *Tam* was glorious,

O'er a' the ills o' life victorious!

   But pleasures are like poppies spread,

You seize the flower, its bloom is shed;

Or like the snow falls in the river,
A moment white — then melts for ever;
Or like the borealis race,
That flit ere you can point their place;
Or like the rainbow's lovely form
Evanishing amid the storm. —
Nae man can tether time or tide;   no, hold/control
The hour approaches *Tam* maun ride;   must
That hour, o' night's black arch the key-stane,   -stone
That dreary hour he mounts his beast in;
And sic a night he taks the road in,   such, takes
As ne'er poor sinner was abroad in.

The wind blew as 'twad blawn its last;   it would have blown
The rattling showers rose on the blast;
The speedy gleams the darkness swallow'd;
Loud, deep, and lang, the thunder bellow'd: long
That night, a child might understand,
The Deil had business on his hand.   devil

Weel mounted on his gray mare, *Meg* —   well
A better never lifted leg —
Tam skelpit on thro' dub and mire,   rode fast, puddle
Despising wind, and rain, and fire;
Whyles holding fast his guid blue bonnet;   good

Whyles crooning o'er some auld Scots sonnet; muttering, old

Whyles glow'ring round wi' prudent cares, looking with fear

Lest bogles catch him unawares: bogies

Kirk-Alloway was drawing nigh, where

Whare ghaists and houlets nightly cry. — ghosts, owls

By this time he was cross the ford, burn

Whare in the snaw the chapman smoor'd; where, snow, pedlar, smothered

And past the birks and meikle stane, birches, big stone

Whare drunken *Charlie* brak's neck-bane; where, broke his, -bone

And thro' the whins, and by the cairn, gorse bushes

Whare hunters fand the murder'd bairn; where, found, child

And near the thorn, aboon the well, above

Whare *Mungo's* mither hang'd hersel. — where, mother

Before him *Doon* pours all his floods;

The doubling storm roars thro' the woods;

The lightnings flash from pole to pole;

Near and more near the thunders roll:

When, glimmering thro' the groaning trees,

Kirk-Alloway seem'd in a bleeze; blaze/lit up

Thro' ilka bore the beams were glancing; every chink in the wall

And loud resounded mirth and dancing.

Inspiring bold *John Barleycorn!*

What dangers thou canst make us scorn!

Wi' tippenny, we fear nae evil;   *cheap two-*
                                       penny ale, no

Wi' usquabae, we'll face the Devil! —   *whisky*

The swats sae ream'd in *Tammie's* noddle,   *small beers,*
                                       so, mind

Fair play, he car'd na deils a boddle.   *cared not a*
                                       farthing

But *Maggie* stood, right sair astonish'd,   *sore*

Till, by the heel and hand admonish'd,   *spurred and*
                                       slapped

She ventur'd forward on the light;

And, vow! *Tam* saw an unco sight!   *strange/*
                                       wondrous

Warlocks and witches in a dance;   *wizards*

Nae cotillion brent new frae *France*,   *no, brand*
                                       new from

But hornpipes, jigs, strathspeys, and reels,

Put life and mettle in their heels.

A winnock-bunker in the east,   *window*
                                       recess

There sat auld Nick, in shape o' beast;   *old*

A tousie tyke, black, grim, and large,   *shaggy dog*

To gie them music was his charge: *give*

He screw'd the pipes and gart them skirl,   *made, blare*

Till roof and rafters a' did dirl. —   *ring/shake*

Coffins stood round, like open presses,

That shaw'd the dead in their last dresses;   *showed*

And by some devilish cantraip sleight,   *magic trick*

Each in its cauld hand held a light. —   *cold*

By which heroic *Tam* was able

To note upon the haly table,   *holy*

A murderer's banes, in gibbet-airns;   *bones, -irons*

Twa span-lang, wee, unchristen'd bairns;   two, -long, babies

A thief new-cutted frae a rape,   from, rope

Wi' his last gasp his gab did gape;   mouth, gasp

Five tomahawks wi' blude red-rusted;   axes, blood

Five scymitars wi' murder crusted;

A garter, which a babe had strangled;

A knife, a father's throat had mangled,

Whom his ain son o' life bereft,   own

The grey-hairs yet stack to the heft;   stuck, handle

[Three Layers' tongues, turned inside out,

Wi' lies seamed like a beggar's clout;

Three Priests' hearts, rotten black as muck,

Lay stinking, vile, in every neuk].   corner

    As *Tammie* glowr'd, amaz'd, and curious,   stared

The mirth and fun grew fast and furious:

The piper loud and louder blew;

The dancers quick and quicker flew;

They reel'd, they set, they cross'd, they cleekit,   clasped one another

Till ilka carlin swat and reekit,   every witch, sweated, steamed

And coost her duddies to the wark,   cast off clothes, work

And linket at it in her sark!   set to it, shirt

Now *Tam*, O *Tam*! had thae been queans, they, girls

A' plump and strapping in their teens,

Their sarks, instead o' creeshie flannen, shirts, greasy flannel

Been snaw-white seventeen hunder linen! snow-, fine threaded linen

Thir breeks o' mine, my only pair, these breeches

That ance were plush, o' guid blue hair, once, good

I wad hae gi'en them off my hurdies, would have given, backside

For ae blink o' the bonie burdies! one, bony lasses

But wither'd beldams, auld and droll, hags, old

Rigwoodie hags wad spean a foal, tough, would, abort

Louping and flinging on a crummock, jumping, cudgel

I wonder did na turn thy stomach. not

But *Tam* kend what was what fu' brawlie, knew, full well

There was ae winsome wench and wawlie, one comely, choice

That night enlisted in the core,

(Lang after kend on *Carrick* shore; long, known

For mony a beast to dead she shot, many

An' perish'd mony a bonie boat, many, bony

And shook baith meikle corn and bear, both much, barley

And kept the country-side in fear).

Her cutty-sark, o' Paisley harn short shirt, coarse cloth

That while a lassie she had worn,

In longitude tho' sorely scanty,   revealing
It was her best, and she was vauntie. —   proud of it
Ah! little kend thy reverend grannie,   knew
That sark she coft for her wee Nannie,   shirt, bought
Wi' twa pund Scots ('twas a' her riches),   two pounds
Wad ever grac'd a dance of witches!   would

But here my Muse her wing maun cour;   must fold/curb
Sic flights are far beyond her pow'r;   such
To sing how Nannie lap and flang,   leaped, kicked
(A souple jad she was, and strang),   supple lass, strong
And how *Tam* stood like ane bewitch'd,   one
And thought his very een enrich'd;   eyes
Even Satan glowr'd, and fidg'd fu' fain,   stared, fidgeted excitedly
And hotch'd and blew wi' might and main: jerked
Till first ae caper, syne anither,   one, then another
Tam tint his reason a' thegither,   lost, together
And roars out, 'Weel done, Cutty-sark!'   well
And in an instant all was dark:
And scarcely had he *Maggie* rallied,
When out the hellish legion sallied.

As bees bizz out wi' angry fyke,   buzz, fret
When plundering herds assail their byke;   hive
As open pussie's mortal foes,   a hare's

When, pop! she starts before their nose;
As eager runs the market-crowd,
When 'Catch the thief!' resounds aloud;
So *Maggie* runs, the witches follow,
Wi' mony an eldritch skriech and hollow.   many, unearthly screech

Ah, *Tam*! ah, *Tam*! thou'll get thy fairin'!   reward/due
In hell they'll roast thee like a herrin'!
In vain thy *Kate* awaits thy comin'!
Kate soon will be a woefu' woman!
Now, do thy speedy utmost, Meg,
And win the key-stane of the brig;   key-stone, bridge
There, at them thou thy tail may toss,
A running stream they dare na cross.   not
But ere the key-stane she could make,   key-stone
The fient a tail she had to shake!   little of
For Nannie, far before the rest,
Hard upon noble *Maggie* prest,   pressed
And flew at *Tam* wi' furious ettle;   aim
But little wist she Maggie's mettle —   was
Ae spring brought off her master hale,   one, whole
But left behind her ain grey tail: own
The carlin claught her by the rump,   old witch caught
And left poor *Maggie* scarce a stump.

Now, wha this tale o' truth shall read,   who
Ilk man and mother's son take heed: each
Whene'er to drink you are inclin'd,
Or cutty-sarks run in your mind,   short shirts/ skirts
Think! ye may buy the joys o'er dear —
Remember *Tam o' Shanter's* mare.

A Man's a Man for a' That

Is there, for honest Poverty
 That hings his head, an' a' that;   *hangs*
The coward-slave, we pass him by,
 We dare be poor for a' that!
For a' that, an' a' that,
 Our toils obscure, an' a' that,
The rank is but the guinea's stamp,
 The Man's the gowd for a' that.   *gold*

What though on hamely fare we dine,   *homely foods*
 Wear hoddin grey, an' a' that?   *coarse woollen cloth*
Gie fools their silks, and knaves their wine,   *give*
 A Man's a Man for a' that.
For a' that, an' a' that,
 Their tinsel show, an' a' that;
The honest man, tho' e'er sae poor,   *so*
 Is king o' men for a' that.

Ye see yon birkie ca'd a lord,   *fellow*
        Wha struts, an' stares, an' a' that,   *called*
Tho' hundreds worship at his word,
        He's but a coof for a' that.   *fool/lout*
For a' that, an' a' that,
        His ribband, star, an' a' that,
The man o' independent mind,
        He looks an' laughs at a' that.

A prince can mak a belted knight,
        A marquis, duke, an' a' that!
But an honest man's aboon his might —   *above*
        Guid faith, he mauna fa' that!   *good, must not be like*
For a' that, an' a' that,
        Their dignities, an' a' that,
The pith o' Sense an' pride o' Worth
        Are higher rank than a' that.

Then let us pray that come it may,
        As come it will for a' that,
That Sense and Worth o'er a' the earth
        Shall bear the gree an' a' that.   *win the day*
For a' that, an' a' that,
        It's comin yet for a' that,
That Man to Man the warld o'er   *world*
        Shall brithers be for a' that.   *brothers*

Such a Parcel of Rogues in a Nation

Fareweel to a' our Scottish fame,   farewell
    Fareweel our ancient glory;
Fareweel even to the Scottish name,
    Sae famed in martial story!   so
Now Sark rins o'er the Solway sands,   runs
    And Tweed rins to the ocean,   runs
To mark whare England's province stands,   where
    Such a parcel of rogues in a nation!

What force or guile could not subdue,
    Thro' many warlike ages,
Is wrought now by a coward few,
    For hireling traitors' wages.
The English steel we could disdain,
    Secure in valour's station;
But English gold has been our bane,
    Such a parcel of rogues in a nation!

O would, or I had seen the day
    That Treason thus could sell us,
My auld grey head had lien in clay,   old, lain
    Wi' BRUCE and loyal WALLACE!
But pith and power, till my last hour,
    I'll mak this declaration;
We're bought and sold for English gold,
    Such a parcel of rogues in a nation!

Westlin Winds

Now westlin winds and slaught'ring guns   from the
                                                      west
    Bring Autumn's pleasant weather;
The moorcock springs on whirring wings
    Amang the blooming heather:
Now waving grain, wide o'er the plain,
    Delights the weary Farmer;
The moon shines bright, as I rove at night
    To muse upon my Charmer.

The Paitrick lo'es the fruitfu' fells,   partridge
                                                      loves
    The Plover lo'es the mountains;
The Woodcock haunts the lanely dells,   lonely
    The soaring Hern the fountains;   heron
                                                    wood
Thro' lofty groves the Cushat roves,   pigeon
    The path o' man to shun it;
The hazel bush o'erhangs the Thrush,
    The spreading thorn the Linnet.

Thus ev'ry kind their pleasure find,
    The savage and the tender;
Some social join, and leagues combine,
    Some solitary wander:
Avaunt, away! the cruel sway,
    Tyrannic man's dominion!
The Sportsman's joy, the murd'ring cry,
    The flutt'ring, gory pinion!

But, PEGGY dear, the ev'ning's clear,
    Thick flies the skimming swallow,
The sky is blue, the fields in view
    All fading-green and yellow:
Come let us stray our gladsome way,
    And view the charms o' Nature;
The rustling corn, the fruited thorn,
    And ilka happy creature.   every

We'll gently walk, and sweetly talk,
    While the silent moon shines clearly;
I'll clasp thy waist, and, fondly prest,
    Swear how I lo'e thee dearly: love
Not vernal show'rs to budding flow'rs,
    Not Autumn to the Farmer,
So dear can be as thou to me,
    My fair, my lovely Charmer!

A Red, Red Rose

O my Luve's like a red, red rose,
    That's newly sprung in June;
O my Luve's like the melodie
    That's sweetly play'd in tune. —

As fair art thou, my bonie lass,
    So deep in luve am I;
And I will luve thee still, my Dear,
    Till a' the seas gang dry. —   go

Till a' the seas gang dry, my Dear,   go
    And the rocks melt wi' the sun:
I will luve thee still, my Dear,
    While the sands o' life shall run. —

And fare thee weel, my only Luve!   well
    And fare thee weel, a while!
And I will come again, my Luve,
    Tho' it were ten thousand mile!

Mary Morison

O Mary, at thy window be,
    It is the wish'd, the trysted hour;
Those smiles and glances let me see,
    That make the miser's treasure poor:
How blythely wad I bide the stoure,   *would, abide, dust/struggle*
    A weary slave frae sun to sun;   *from*
Could I the rich reward secure,
    The lovely Mary Morison!

Yestreen when to the trembling string   *yesterday evening*
    The dance gaed thro' the lighted ha',   *went, hall*
To thee my fancy took its wing,
    I sat, but neither heard or saw:
Though this was fair, and that was braw,   *fine/good looking*
    And yon the toast of a' the town,   *an other, all*
I sigh'd, and said amang them a',   *among, all*
    'Ye are na Mary Morison.'   *you are not*

O Mary, canst thou wreck his peace,
    Wha for thy sake wad gladly die!   who, would
Or canst thou break that heart of his,
    Whase only faut is loving thee!   fault
If love for love thou wilt na gie,   will not give
    At least be pity to me shown;
A thought ungentle canna be   cannot be
    The thought o' Mary Morison.

Ae Fond Kiss

Ae fond kiss, and then we sever;   one
Ae fareweel, and then forever!   one
Deep in heart-wrung tears I'll pledge thee,
Warring sighs and groans I'll wage thee. —

Who shall say that Fortune grieves him,
While the star of hope she leaves him:
Me, nae cheerfu' twinkle lights me;   no
Dark despair around benights me. —

I'll ne'er blame my partial fancy:
Naething could resist my Nancy: nothing
But to see her, was to love her;
Love but her, and love for ever. —

Had we never lov'd sae kindly,   so
Had we never lov'd sae blindly!   so
Never met — or never parted,
We had ne'er been broken-hearted. —

Fare-thee-weel, thou first and fairest!   -well
Fare-thee-weel, thou best and dearest!
Thine be ilka joy and treasure,   each/every
Peace, Enjoyment, Love and Pleasure! —

Ae fond kiss, and then we sever!
Ae fareweel, Alas, for ever!
Deep in heart-wrung tears I'll pledge thee,
Warring sighs and groans I'll wage thee. —

Auld Lang Syne

Should auld acquaintance be forgot   old
    And never brought to mind?
Should auld acquaintance be forgot,
    And auld lang syne!   long ago

Chorus
For auld lang syne, my jo,   friend
    For auld lang syne,
We'll tak a cup o' kindness yet
    For auld lang syne.

And surely ye'll be your pint stowp!   pay for
    And surely I'll be mine!
And we'll tak a cup o' kindness yet,
    For auld lang syne.
        For auld lang syne, &c.

We twa hae run about the braes,   two,
    And pou'd the gowans fine;   hillsides
                              pulled,
                              daisies

But we've wander'd mony a weary fitt,   many, foot
    Sin auld lang syne.
        For auld lang syne, &c.

We twa hae paidl'd in the burn,   two have
                                                         paddled
    Frae morning sun till dine;   from
But seas between us braid hae roar'd,   broad have
    Sin auld lang syne.
        For auld lang syne, &c.

And there's a hand, my trusty fiere!   companion
    And gie's a hand o' thine!   give me
And we'll tak a right gude-willie-waught,   good-will
                                                         drink
    For auld lang syne!
        For auld lang syne, &c.

CANONGATE CLASSICS

Books listed in alphabetical order by author:

The Life of Robert Burns Catherine Carswell
  ISBN 0 86241 292 7 £6.99
Lying Awake Catherine Carswell
  ISBN 0 86241 683 3 £5.99
Open the Door! Catherine Carswell
  ISBN 0 86241 644 2 £5.99
The Triumph Tree: Scotland's Earliest Poetry 550–1350
  Thomas Owen Clancy (ed.)
  ISBN 0 86241 787 2 £9.99
Twentieth-Century Scottish Drama: An Anthology
  Craig/Stevenson (eds)
  ISBN 0 86241 979 4 £12.99
Two Worlds David Daiches
  ISBN 0 86241 704 X £5.99
The Complete Brigadier Gerard Arthur Conan Doyle
  ISBN 0 86241 534 9 £6.99
A Glasgow Trilogy George Friel
  ISBN 086241 885 2 £9.99
Dance of the Apprentices Edward Gaitens
  ISBN 0 86241 297 8 £7.99
Ringan Gilhaize John Galt
  ISBN 0 86241 552 7 £6.99
The Member and the Radical John Galt
  ISBN 0 86241 642 6 £5.99
Memoirs of a Highland Lady vols I & II
Elizabeth Grant of Rothiemurchus
  ISBN 0 86241 396 6 £8.99

The Three Perils of Man James Hogg
   ISBN 0 86241 646 9 £8.99
Flemington & Tales from Angus Violet Jacob
   ISBN 0 86241 784 8 £8.99
Fergus Lamont Robin Jenkins
   ISBN 0 86241 310 9 £6.99
Just Duffy Robin Jenkins
   ISBN 0 86241 551 9 £5.99
The Changeling Robin Jenkins
   ISBN 0 86241 228 5 £5.99
Journey to the Hebrides (A Journey to the Western Isles
of Scotland, The Journal of a Tour to the Hebrides)
   Samuel Johnson & James Boswell
   ISBN 0 86241 588 8 £6.99
Household Ghosts: A James Kennaway Omnibus
(Tunes of Glory, Household Ghosts, Silence)
   James Kennaway
   ISBN 1 84195 125 0 £7.99
Wisdom, Madness and Folly RD Laing
   ISBN 0 86241 831 3 £5.99
The Haunted Woman David Lindsay
   ISBN 0 86241 162 9 £6.99
A Voyage to Arcturus David Lindsay
   ISBN 0 86241 377 X £6.99
Ane Satyre of the Thrie Estaitis Sir David Lindsay
   ISBN 0 86241 191 2 £4.99
The Dark of Summer Eric Linklater
   ISBN 0 86241 894 1 £5.99

Magnus Merriman Eric Linklater
ISBN 0 86241 313 3 £6.99
Private Angelo Eric Linklater
ISBN 0 86241 376 1 £5.99
Scottish Ballads Emily Lyle (ed.)
ISBN 0 86241 477 6 £5.99
Nua-Bhardachd Ghaidhlig/Modern Scottish Gaelic Poems
   Donald MacAulay (ed.)
ISBN 0 86241 494 6 £4.99
The Early Life of James McBey James McBey
ISBN 0 86241 445 8 £5.99
Three Scottish Poets MacCaig, Morgan, Lochhead
ISBN 0 86241 400 8 £6.99
And the Cock Crew Fionn MacColla
ISBN 0 86241 536 5 £4.99
The Devil and the Giro: Two Centuries of Scottish Stories
   Carl MacDougall (ed.)
ISBN 0 86241 359 1 £9.99
St Kilda: Island on the Edge of the World Charles Maclean
ISBN 0 86241 388 5 £6.99
Linmill Stories Robert McLellan
ISBN 0 86241 282 X £6.99
Homeward Journey John MacNair Reid
ISBN 0 86241 178 5 £3.95
The Silver Bough F. Marian McNeill
ISBN 0 86241 231 5 £6.99
Wild Harbour Ian Macpherson
ISBN 0 86241 234 X £6.99

A Childhood in Scotland Christian Miller
ISBN 0 86241 230 7 £4.99

The Blood of the Martyrs Naomi Mitchison
ISBN 0 86241 192 0 £8.99

The Corn King and the Spring Queen Naomi Mitchison
ISBN 0 86241 287 0 £9.99

The Gowk Storm Nancy Brysson Morrison
ISBN 0 86241 222 6 £4.99

An Autobiography Edwin Muir
ISBN 0 86241 423 7 £6.99

The Wilderness Journeys (The Story of My Boyhood and
    Youth, A Thousand Mile Walk to the Gulf, My First
    Summer in the Sierra, Travels in Alaska, Stickeen)
    John Muir
    ISBN 0 86241 586 1 £9.99

Imagined Selves: (Imagined Corners, Mrs Ritchie, Mrs
    Grundy in Scotland, Women: An Inquiry, Women in
    Scotland) Willa Muir
    ISBN 0 86241 605 1 £8.99

A Beleaguered City: Tales of the Seen and Unseen
    Margaret Oliphant
    ISBN 1 84195 060 2 £7.99

A Twelvemonth and a Day Christopher Rush
    ISBN 0 86241 439 3 £6.99

The End of an Old Song J.D. Scott
    ISBN 0 86241 311 7 £4.95

The Journal of Sir Walter Scott WEK Anderson (ed.)
    ISBN 0 86241 828 3 £12.99

The Bad Sister: An Emma Tennant Omnibus (The Bad
  Sister, Two Women of London, Wild Nights)
  Emma Tennant
  ISBN 1 84195 053 X £7.99
The People of the Sea David Thomson
  ISBN 1 84195 107 2 £6.99
The City of Dreadful Night James Thomson
  ISBN 0 86241 449 0 £5.99
Black Lamb and Grey Falcon Rebecca West
  ISBN 0 86241 428 8 £12.99
The King and the Lamp: Scottish Traveller Tales
  Duncan and Linda Williamson
  ISBN 1 84195 063 7 £7.99